Reflections and Sunsets

Copyright Hoffman Aipira 2006

All rights reserved. No part of this publication may be reproduced, stored in a retrieval system, or transmitted in any form or by any means, electronic, mechanical, photocopying, recording or otherwise, without prior permission from the publishers.

Published by
Kachere Series
P.O. Box 1037, Zomba, Malawi

ISBN 99908-76-60-6 (Kachere Books no. 25) ISBN-13: 978-99908-76-60-4

The Kachere Series is represented outside Africa by
African Books Collective, Oxford, UK (orders@africanbookscollective.com)
Michigan State University Press, East Lansing, MI, USA (msupress@msu.edu)

Layout and Cover Design: Caroline Chihana

Printed by Lightning Source

Reflections and Sunsets

Hoffman Aipira

Kachere Books no. 25

Kachere Series
Zomba
2006

Kachere Series
P.O. Box 1037, Zomba, Malawi
kachere@globemw.net
www.sndp.org.mw/kachereseries/

This book is part of the Kachere Series, a range of books on religion, culture and society from Malawi. Other Kachere books are:

Anthony Nazombe, *Operations and Tears. A New Anthology of Malawian Poetry*

Pia Thielmann, *Love and other Improbabilities*

Pia Thielmann, *Hotbed. Black and White Love in Novels from the United States, Africa, and the Caribbean*

Ernst Wendland, *Sewero. Christian Drama and the Drama of Christianity in Africa*

Masiye Tembo, *Touched by His Grace. A Ngoni Story of Tragedy and Triumph*

Orison Ian Boma Mkandawire, *Face to Face with my Life*

Andy G Khumbanyiwa, *Better Days Around the Corner. Restoration of Hope, Self-Confidence and the Desire to Succeed*

Orison Ian Boma Mkandawire, *Chiswakhata Mkandawire of Livingstonia*

The Kachere Series is the publications arm of the Department of Theology and Religious Studies of the University of Malawi.

Series Editors: J.C. Chakanza, F.L. Chingota, Klaus Fiedler, P.A. Kalilombe
C Katumbi, S. Mahommad, Fulata Moyo, Martin Ott

Acknowledgements

Are due to the editors of the following publications where some of these poems were first published: *Upstart!* (Milton Keynes, UK) for 'The Hills of Kabula' and 'The Buzz on a Tropical Beach;' *Illuminations (*South Carolina, USA), for 'Another Winter', 'When the Sun Went Down on a Serpent,' 'Through a Down Pour' and 'Fireflies;' *Dream Catcher,* (York & Lincoln, UK), for 'The Flood,' 'The First Rains' and 'Last Orders;' *MAU* (London), for 'Distant Drums' and *The Shop* (Ireland), for 'Two Halves,' 'At Wenela Bus Station' and 'Crossing Continents.'

Several other poems were included in: *Operations and Tears, New Anthology of Malawian Poetry*, Kachere Series (2004), edited by Anthony Nazombe. And two poems were published by *The Royal Festival Hall,* London, in 2003, as part of the UK Poetry digitization project.

Hoffman Aipira
York, England.

Contents

I. Reflections and Sunsets
The First Rains	9
Dad	10
At Wenela Bus Station	11
Reflections	12
Sunset at Lake Malawi	13
High Winds at Mpale	14
The View from Bunda Hill	16
The Hills of Kabula	17
New Landscapes, New Lives	18
Mix and Match	19
The Last Respects	20
Fireflies	21
New Dispensation Malawi, 1996	22
The Buzz on a Tropical Beach	23

II. Another Winter
Crossing Continents	25
Waiting for Pelicans, St James's Park	26
Midsummer, North Yorkshire, England	27
Cambridge	28
An Evening on the City	29
Nocturnal Shadows	30
Another Winter	31
Last Orders	32

III. Distant Drums
Through a Downpour, Chikwawa Road	34
Two Halves	35
Distant Drums	36
Grandfather's Footsteps	37
When the Sun Went Down on a Serpent	39
Untitled	40
Departing Kwekwe, Zimbabwe 1975	41
Elegies	42

IV. Telling Tales
Chichiri 3pm	45
Telling Tales	46
The Granaries at Kanengo	47
The Mtondo Trees of Mangochi	48
The Cenotaph on Chipembere Highway	49
Those Makungwa Nights	50
Visiting Maone	51

Not I	52
The Flood, Mozambique 2000	50
Facing Zomba Plateau	54
Notes and glossary	55

I. Reflections and Sunsets

The First Rains

A curtain of darkness drops.
Engulfing day into night, it creeps
Through blank windows, swells up
Inside blinking eyes, blurring vision.

Trees sigh in the widening night.
Chickens, cooing eerily,
Gather their young under feathers,
And dogs curl like commas by fireplaces.

In the distance, thunderous clouds
Scatter lightning like fireworks
Across jittery skies. Suddenly,
North wind drives down first rains

And we talk of the smell of wet earth rising
Of upland gullies and springs flowing into
Mainstreams, of young birds and insects trying
New wings on the bustling pages of the veld.

Dad

Take the hoe my son
Carefully tie the seed-bag
At the end of the hoe-handle.
At first light
Before the dew is dry
Mark a patch of soil
To carry this seed
And give life
Hope.

At Wenela Bus Station, 1997
    for Lawrence Vilili

And here we come and go, arrive and depart,
Travellers journeying to and fro, buses and mini
Buses loading and offloading their human cargo
Amid deafening engine noise and stiff turpentine
Scents of eucalyptus trees perfuming the air.

Then the grinding to a halt of wheels, of doors
Slammed shut or left ajar, the squeaking to life
Of stuttering engines and a long peep! followed
By final messages dancing on people's lips.

On the tarmac, a driver slowly changing gear, revving
The engine prompts vigorous arm waving, thudding
Against plate glass windows. But standing here today,
I am reminded of dear friends long departed, their smiles
And handshakes vivid on the mystic walls of memory.

Reflections, Mvumba Village

(i)

Mango trees laying out flowers and
Wealthy in foliage, fragrance and pollinators
Buzz with bees, pollen-happy, hovering and
Landing on bluish-creamy florets. The trees
Will prosper. Remembering last year's fruit,
We set sights beyond the bee's spectacle
To trees fruiting heavily and nature's sugars
Racing through stems, fortifying in ripening
Mangoes, sweetening that November.

(ii)

After a light smattering of rain
Father and son gleaming with sweat
Heel watermelon seeds in ridges.
A brown sparrow in thick undergrowth
Breaks cover, twittering a mating melody
A wild romantic cry tinged with apprehension.
Meanwhile, the father, his feet slowing with weariness
Whistles a tune, some *Kwela* music perhaps
Remembered from another time.

(iii)

February passes into March without a pause.
We wait another season of maize, sorghum
And millet; harvested, fermented and brewed
Into *thobwa*. Working best on stomachs full
Of the sweet brew, we will join hands and wade
Through *dimba* gardens rampant with weeds, hoeing
And planting short season crops for *mfutso*
Like our forefathers had done before.

Sunset at Lake Malawi
   for Robert Kawiya

Wisdom, they say, is to know
The harmony of things, and Joy
Is to dance to their rhythm.
At Malembo harbour, the lake
Mirroring golden-bright skies above
Glows and sparkles like a sea
Of gold. The lake exhaling gently
Sends low waves out and back, one
After the other, soft as a whisper.

A lone fisherman launching his dugout canoe
Onto calm waters, paddles solo
Past water-marked rocks
Beyond colonies of reeds
Alive with a cacophony of songs,
Frogs and crickets singing like a hastily
Assembled choir, entertaining
Themselves for hours on end.

I sit on the water's edge
In the gentler heat of the day,
Freshly roasted maize-on-the cob
Between my teeth, watching
The setting sun, a softened red ball
Climbing down the sky and retiring
Below shimmering Funwe mountain.

But my attention is drawn to flocks
Of migrating birds in their thousands
Thickening and suddenly simplifying
Their lines in the pathless air. Their
Senses honed from the beginning of time,
Their flight path governed by the orbit
Of stars, and the moon's procession
Pacing the lake slowly onto golden
Grains of sand that carpet Malembo harbour.

High Winds at Mpale, 1980

I have known lake Malawi
Raise its voice in tidal waves
Flogging the shoreline.

Little did I expect lake Malombe
Minuscule by comparison
To march landward angrily.
Hard to believe this tranquil
Lake would one day
Be woken up by high winds
Preceding a thunderstorm -
Fierce waves like thunders
Belching from the lakebed
The waves roaring, tormenting the shore
Battering reed-beds as if to extract
Confession from the hollow stems.

Over CheChimwala village, the pelting winds
Whacking trees and houses mercilessly
Swept fisheagles northwards
Sowing the skies with sticks and stones,
Dry straw, feathers and dust
Blown from all directions, mixed
And matched and abandoned on the ground.

It was not until late afternoon
That the cool touch of the evening breeze
Blowing freely through shattered windows
Brought families out with pained faces.
Eyes red with uncried tears they surveyed
The footprints of tempestuous power of
The elements: dismantled roofs, waterweeds
Unfastened from the lakebed, torn drift nets,
Algae-coated crumbling driftwood and

Frames of fishing boats and dugout
Canoes smashed and twisted -

The damage systematic and brutal.
In the depth of this loss, the destructive
Lake lying calm and the high winds dissipating,
Who among us will comfort and explain
The Love and Charity of God?

The View from Bunda Hill

Bunda Hill, the way you preside over
The college grounds, stone-faced, half-hidden
By *Brachystegia* woodland; the trees obeying
The whistling wind swaying in applause –

Conceals your bitter history that still haunts
Lives here. Mother Bunda, your unlit caves
Were death-beds for waves of *Akafulas*
Who perished in your womb, overwhelmed

By woodsmoke in a hellish fire furnace of
Flesh, bones and wood, as hostile *Ngonis*
Incinerated *Akafulas* to death. Their demise
Is carried in poet's lines and *Chewa* folklore.

Bunda Hill, today a stream of literature runs
Below you, feeding and nourishing students
Slogging their way through a forest of books
Busily printing data into their smart memory.

The significance of this is not lost during
The Finals, when heads lean over answer sheets
And sharpened pens and minds do the talking
In the invigilated silence of the exam room.

The Hills of Kabula

Those hills and lofty peaks in sweltering midday heat
Were covered in green once. Pristine streams snaked
Downhill, crashing melodiously on rocky falls.

I remember birds of a feather sharpened chisel beaks
On *Masuku* fruits; plump and ripe on the vine as tap
Roots muscled through virgin earth with patient labour.

Today the hills stand still, without green insulation
Without the crackling chorus of mature trees and
The see-sawing lyrics of exuberant birdlife - and I grieve.

New Cities, New Landscapes

The globe fast forwards
To a massive construction site.
Temples of brick and mortar
Speak in landmarks.
Emerging cities a concrete jungle
Asserting itself.

The fizzy voice of celebration
Pops out champagne bottles
An icing on ribbon cutting rituals,
Handshakes and mouth-wide grins.

Somewhere on the globe
Cranes and shovels
Club together in union
Like promiscuous earth diggers
Lifting up with rising expectations
On virgin lands.

Falling on the debris
Generous heavens disperse
Drizzly rain like friendly arsenals
Torturing our senses
With dry scent of cement.

Those who care about green
Notice anorexic trees tottering
Into ubiquitous skyline
Gasping for air.
A mature forest nearby
Grunts, shedding leaves
Before the autumn fall

Mix and Match

Look at these superhighways
On desktops, post-modern towers
Mushrooming and choicest palate
Onto dinner tables gobbled
By gold-plated false teeth.

This is the new world
Lighting candles here, casting shadows there
And there:

Caviar lingering under silver chandeliers
A la Carte meals wafting aromatic scents
And well cropped chins jutting out
In bold aftershave – Not a sniff.

Chinaware made-to-order
Cutlery on a bed of velvet serviettes
And diamonds glittering
On women's necklines – Not in sight.

Of the craftsmen in chef hats
Tending pans of crispy salads
And flaming grills shouldering
Rare steaks – Only hardwork
Heat and overtime.

The Last Respects

Death falls on sudden wings
And a graveyard plays host
To faces of anguish,
Eyes watching fingers
Tears rolling
Down sagging chins.

In the midst of solemnity
A village priest mutters the last rites
As the deceased exits
To a callous void
Without best wishes.

From a tired amber sky
A fading face of the sunset
Observes
Shovels and spades
Attacking earth mounds
Burying difficult times.

Fireflies

Between the earth and sky, the night is still.
A crackle of dry twigs in the mango tree
And our guard dog *Sauzana* wailing
At something or the other in the dark
Breaks the stillness. Then, out of nowhere
Fireflies swarm the night like neon lamps.
You'd think it was a starry night
The fireflies flickering
Against the moonless face of the night
A dazzling display of bluish-green illumination -
Pure poetry of lighting effects.
Children filled with wonder brave
The night, marvelling at fireflies
Flashing noiselessly, straying like nomads.
I cup a few into my curious hands
A tiny collection, each fragile as infants,
But a big prize for childhood curiosity.

New Dispensation, Malawi 1996
for Boniface Dulani

We've seen those men before, clad in
Amulets and anklets, animal skins and
Colourful feathers; stabbing the air in full
Battle cry, ancestral shields and spears
Menacing, the feet thundering the ground
Traditional songs peaking, dancing *ingoma*.

We've talked about *beni* dancing troupe
Their rehearsed dance steps so uniform
Their nimbler footwork mesmerising
Quickening to the beat of the master drum.
The women in bright *chitenje* ululating
Choking the air with monotonous chants.

We've blabbed about men and women
Crowding beer halls, ordering packets
Of *Chibuku* beer, warm and shaken
Carefully passed from lip to lip between
Fear-tinged conversation, coded questions
And beer-rich laughter lifting low spirits.

That was years ago. Today at Kamba
Bottle store complex, the *Naperi* River
Nearby murmuring in its stone-pimpled
Path; the drinking gentry whose numbers
Swell with the supply of dewed Carlsbergs
Mutter in flat voices about the nouveau riche.

Tattered yester-lives today's tycoons zooming
In gleaming 4x4's. I hear men bewildered by red
Lipstick concubines and their lovers, two by two
As if going to Noah's Ark, busily unwrapping
Like fast food behind closed doors. New dispensation
Certainly. But haven't we been here before?

The Buzz on a Tropical Beach

At the golden sands beach
The expansive blue lake
Clear in its ebb and flow, beckons
The sun sparkling in the waves
And visitors stepping out
Of their clothes into sun tan lotions.

The tenderized skin of a playful couple
In a mouth to mouth resuscitation
Is an oasis for mosquitoes.

With the outdoors warm
And passions rising,
A fan blowing cool in an
Outlandish mock Tudor bar
Draws me to a piercing gaze
From the bar lady.

Weighing the psychology
Of the moment, I stand transfixed
Swatting a mosquito, buzzing
Me loud like the echoes
For last orders.

II. Another Winter

Crossing Continents
   for John Kudjoe

Do you remember the harsh English winters
Freezing our illusion of lovely sabbatical?
Do you remember walking ice-capped roads
And pavements, the mercury on the thermometer
Thawing, the earth slowly shedding its new
Frozen silver skin, revealing junipers in the park
Still holding on to their needles among leafless
Fuschias and dog rose? Do you remember
The children on the mound snow boarding, screaming
With triumphant joy as they hurtled down slope
To nowhere? Don't you remember young couples
Dog walking, hurling snowballs at each other
In mock fights and tossing a bone of contention
In the air for a golden spaniel to fetch?

Remember kick-starting our dear-selves into long
Debates about the endless arctic spells here, our snow-
Bitten fingers and toes stuffed deep inside padded
Pockets and thermal socks as if in suspended animation?
But as you depart for the sun-drenched tropics
Memories come cascading: pots of *fufu* and *nsima*
Bubbling ferociously to warm your palate; of kith and kin
Imbibing gourdfuls of palm wine and *apelteshie* amid
The lengthy greetings of home, celebrating your arrival.

Waiting for Pelicans, St James's Park, London
    for Raymond Swaray

Clusters of daffodils peep out here and there
Through verdant lawn. The flowers bright-yellow
Like wall paper gold on a grassy bank, where
Morsels of food fly off my hands to feed
A family of ducks massing, expecting a bribe
Pocketing the breadcrumbs into their beaks.

Above my head, pelicans gliding on a cushion
Of air come down to land on duck-stirred lake
Drawn perhaps by curiosity, their feet tucked
In a pillow of feathers, screw-necked even.

I lob a few crumbs in their direction, the ducks
Rapid response retrieving the food in mid-air.
More attempts pass unnoticed. The pelicans'
Blank stare is unanimous as if to say -
"Food isn't what we are about here."

Midsummer, North Yorkshire, England
   for Diana Favre

At the height of the tourist season
In June and July, find time and visit
Burnby Hall Gardens and Museum
Near Pocklington in North Yorkshire.
When the museum's sprawling gardens
Are lush with vegetation, and the roofs
Of the upper and lower lakes are afloat
With blooming water lilies, launch pads
For froglets executing acrobatic dive like
Tiny U.F.O's into the belly of the lake.
Join the crowd in knee-lengths shorts and
Dresses; cones of ice cream in one hand
And mementoes in the other, and make
Your way to the rose bushes, a forest of
Colour and fragrance, unlike the early
Flowering trees, dropping their blossom
To the ground, dressing down for autumn.

Cambridge
    for Ru Li

The River Cam drifts quietly with tourists
Their zoom lenses pointing at the backs
Of Cambridge Colleges, cameras-clicking
Capturing Gothic spires forking sea blue skies.

We take our time and roll the narrow boat
Slowly and surely as if we were
The last visitors here. Another boat-load
Of tourists elbows ours gently away
Sparking fresh blasts of giggles.

And off we went, punting casually.
The light wind blowing assisting
Our sail down river, under humped
Footbridge, one of many; past
Wind-ruffled willows holding
Their heads under the slow waters.

What brings all this to mind are the boats
On York's River Ouse full of tourists
Sailing along the city's medieval landmarks
The face of its past. "It's like looking
Into another life and another world,"
Someone said, eyes catching a glimpse
Of ancient city walls and York Minster
Towering solidly over the city's skyline
Surrounded by UK preservation order.

An Evening on the City
   for Ernest Misomali

The 10.45 Dublin to London plane taxis
On the tarmac, on time. After check-out
Formalities and a short shuttle through
The arrivals gates of cosmopolitan Heathrow,
You head towards the waiting lounge, greeted by
Blinking neon signs and the hum of passengers
Arriving and departing, jetting in and out of
One bitter cold London January.

So here we are, you homeward-bound, transiting
Through London, and me emerging from the Tube
The delayed Piccadilly Line. My eyes scanning
The crowd trying to catch yours on our first
Encounter after years and time zones apart.
Greetings exchanged, we compare old notes,
Wallowing in how much water has gone under
The bridge. Memories are more important
Than history - that one later.

After checking-in at The County for bed &
Breakfast, we stroll down town along shop
Fronts of vast departmental stores, bargain
Hunting the dwindling January sales, stopping
For a nibble and a bite here, a drink there. Our
Conversation flowing back into yester-years
As though time had suddenly reversed its course.

Walking the city streets, the London plane trees
Leafless in the grip of winter, and unlike us,
Travelling light; we faced wintry rain of snow and
More snow falling over the city's skyline, highways
And byways; caking buildings, trees and the tarmac
In snow-white like a new bride. Muffling London's
5pm rush hour squeal. For much needed warmth,
We enter the first open pub accompanied by
Fresh snow, and warmed up, we raise glasses.
Of perfect Guinness clinking with *Cheers!*

Nocturnal Shadows
    for Jack Mapanje

The name of your village Kadango
On the eastern bank of Lake Malawi
Chimes with people's names in my village
Nestling calmly on the lake's western bank.
The vast calendar lake (three hundred and
Sixty five miles long, fifty-two miles wide)
Straddling the land assumes graceful calm,
Almost regal under a tide of moonlight.
Glittering in starlit night like a sea of pearls.

And us? We touch base in the Pennines
Away from palm-fringed beaches of Chigawe.
The wintry mist lifting, we rake a groundswell
Of memories for what might have been. Mulling
Over this, that and the other. Reflecting with
Heavy hearts how manufactured accidents and
Deaths under the pretext of lethal mosquito bite
Thinned the ranks of our countrymen.

And what National covenant did you break
For the Special Branch to comb your path
All hours? Decode and ban your cryptic verse?
Was it the revelatory power of metaphors
Embedded in the lines? The haunting stories
Perhaps? Or the poet in you? And what on God's
Earth did the Chameleon do or fail to do,
To bask blissfully in brilliant African colours
Of camouflage, merging with the rich Nubian
Brownness of its soils, while snailing cautiously
From leafing branch, to dry twig to stone?

No matter. Even when playing safe was instinctive
And natural as a sleeper turning under blankets,
We saw men and women punished for no crimes.
Where the simple act of writing, placing verbs
Between nouns was not an innocent business.

Another Winter
    for Patrick Makina

It's another winter here, the season
Of snowman and minor avalanches
On rooftops; tenacious winds hold
Your breath and the sun suddenly

Illuminates but refuses to warm;
Litterbags queue with their bulging
Frustration of this throw-away society
While empty beer bottles yawn

And cuddle in the cold telling tales
Of wild goings-on in the flats above.
It's winter here, the season of weeping
Nostrils and soaking handkerchiefs;

Although nothing is more unsettling
Than the wind from beans on toast and
The warm beer on tap; but, I gather during
This leave of my absence new *Chiperoni*

Whirlwinds have unleashed green crocodiles
There with mischievous humour frolicking
In our freshly found liberation? Still;

Memories of smoked *chambo* fish linger
Children milling around the dawn fires
And stoking the flames with mango twigs
On the bronzed beaches of the lake.

Last Orders
    for Charles Mwansambo

"Maybe they are some of them students
Getting qualifications at the university
Know what I mean? They all come
Here after studies to finish off
The day, still mouthing book talk
And God knows what, don't they?"

At the Yates's Wine Lodge, the locals
Nursing swift-emptying pints of their
Favourite tipple, exchange quick glances
With students surrounding a table
Spread with beer bottles; the air
Heavy with cigarette smoke
Tittle-tattle and laughter.

At the bar, seasoned punters
Crowding the counter
Drinking themselves silly
Busily flick fivers to the bar tender
And in thick accents bellow-
"A pint of the usual love!"

With a glass of beer in my hand, I take
A seat next to the jukebox blaring out
Seventies numbers. After admiring
Its full head, after a long sip of it, and
With opulent flavours of the brew
Still lingering in my mouth, I think
To myself - "Well, it's my pint after all
And whatever I do or how I drink
This beer is my own business."

III. Distant Drums

Through a Downpour, Chikwawa Road
   for Elias Mbvukuta

Driving through rainy day, between lightning
And restless thunder, I trail sugar-laden
Vehicles tortoising up the escarpment.
The heavy downpour washing the tarmac.

The road rising and falling zigzags through
Rock faces, hillsides carved out and bulldozed
Into narrow stone corridor. Along roadsides
Mangoes yellow with ripeness dangle like lamps.

Driving through hairpin bends, the thunder
Deepening its voice; vehicles eroding
The distance groaned in the wet, while wipers
Danced like puppets on windscreens.

Two Halves

Nightlong, sheets of rainwater hammer
Shacks like an old typewriter. With daybreak
The hammering ceases, another pounding ensues -
The familiar gravel-crunching footsteps, men flocking
To the city for work in the soft light of early morning.

Leaving behind, huts wiped clean by rain shine
In the radiant morning sun. While nameless new
Settlements proliferating along rivers of stinking shit
Greet new citizens, building their past with toil
And hope, and the future with the same.

Half a mile apart, but two worlds away; the other half
Sleep and snore tunefully, cocooned in fine linen
And thick mattresses; dreaming of well-watered
Lawns, angling in municipal reservoirs and
A hole in one on velvet green golf course.

Distant Drums
    for Helen Lee

Look at these masked dancers
In rugged regalia

Trooping out of their *dambwe*
To the melodies of distant drums

Talking in tongues we will never know
But evoking strong passion from the initiated.

It's been like this for generations
Whoever is uninitiated in their traditional rites

Must stay away lest they face ruthless axes.
Have you thought for a while Naomi?

Have you wondered why there is
Initiation for our survival?

Here we are in the cracking heat of the savannah
This kitchen our hide-out. Hold your nerve,

Steady on, Naomi, hold the child
As the masked dancers under the cool ambience

Of a baobab tree leave the air pregnant
With sweat and dust, dancing the big dance.

Grandfather's Footsteps

I'll shoulder my grandfather's metal trap
And follow his footsteps,
Bow and arrow slung across my waist -
Deadly companions.

I'll trace well-worn footpaths
To the majestic Phirilongwe mountain.
On reaching the hillside, I'll
Mark a spot to bury the trap, careful

Like a surgeon locating a vein
Vibrating with life.
I'll look for footprints, hoof-strong
In the ground or pungent smell

Of wildebeests hanging in the air.
I'll unload the trap and settle
Down to the task at hand:
Digging a trap-size hole

To take the monster sunny-side up.
I'll cover the hole with fresh earth
Smoothening and marrying the top
With the surrounding ground.

In a final act, I'll litter the top
With twigs and leaves. I'll part
My chest with two crisscrossing swipes
Motioning prayer.

This is how grandfather and great grandfather
Daring hunters
Blazed trails through forbidding
Thickets and undergrowth

To bring home game;
Oblivious to snakes crawling with menace.
But I'll wait for the drizzling light of day
To light my path.

With the sun toasting my back, I'll re-visit
The trap anticipating a warthog, impala or
Gazelle going to God knows where,
Motionless, like a fallen angel in devil's pit.

When the Sun Went Down on a Serpent

The serpent of savanna, you roamed
These horizons once, the V on your tongue
Flickering, stirring still-air.

You stalked heat-vacuumed valleys,
Criss-crossed sprawling grasslands
And slithered through dense thickets.

We dreaded your glistening fangs,
How they hissed and slanted with venom
Anchoring fatal pain, like precision arrows
Deep into pulsating veins.

We feared the resolute energies
Of your jaws; how they flexed with rage
And flung wide your petite mouth
To devour much larger prey.

Now the potent fangs gone
Was your unflagging bile worth our grief?
Worth the excessive venom?
And where did it get *You*?

Untitled

        I pounded this earth many moon years ago,
My sweat-licked back hunched
Over my hoe, the soil wet with last night's rain; my
Hands cascading, breaking the flat lie
Of the land into corrugations of ridges swollen with
              Unborn generation of seed maize.
Furrow to furrow, feathers ruffled: garden birds
              On chickens, chickens on chickens
Frantic, squabbling over this year's hatch of earthworms,
Dung beetles and scorpions turfed out;
Each thrust of my hoe, unearthing more subterranean life
And musty earthy aroma trapped in rich loam.
Among thick weeds, shaggy grass and colonies of stinging
Nettle I sank the hoe deep, lacerating fibrous
Roots networking underground and saplings sprouting in the wind.
        Today, when I see robust young men indifferent
            To the Hoe and the Pen - the mind boggles.

Departing Kwekwe, Zimbabwe 1975
   for Katie

We lose the early morning lie-in
For a ticket and a seat on the train
Departing Kwekwe station. Arriving
Hours well ahead of time, fingers stiff
With the morning chill, jaws shivering,
The teeth rattled crazily.

On the hour, the journey began
With the station master's final whistle
Blowing us homewards. The train
Tearing itself free from the platform
With a surge and creak of carriages
Rocking us forward, later gathering
Speed, surging northward noisily
Bound for Mutare and lands beyond.

One by one, lamp posts and telegraph
Poles sped past the window. Peering out
Our eyes locked onto the fading figures
Of mother and father waving in the far distance,
The platform almost empty of faces. We were
A little sad that the train had snatched us
A few months after in another country.

Away from Kwekwe station, we sank
Into our seats, rehearsing our newly
Acquired foreign tongue, musing
Over their *sadza* and *m'Bida* being as
Tasty as our *nsima* and *bonongwe*.

An overnight trans-Zambezi crossing after
All change at Mutare and Dondo saw us
Into the familiar landscapes of home, where
A thick scent of the delicious stick-skewered
Smoked *chambo*, urged us home.

(i)

It's years now since you departed.
And though you'll never come back
I am comforted by memories of daylong walks
We took in Kwekwe town, browsing the shops
For new clothes to fit my budding frame.
The shopkeepers smiling at us, smiling
At the thought of converting goods to profit.

Looking back, I recall the Sunday mornings
As you went about your calling, reading
Scriptures behind the pulpit, preaching
The gospel according to Presbyterian faith.
The congregation in their Sunday best
Paying attention to matters of life and
Afterlife, under the gaze of the Almighty.

Years later, lying awake in the small hours
Of daybreak, the cold light of dawn purpling
The east; I try to make sense of life's deep
Meaning and deeper purpose as I recall
The Sundays when Amaveni Church
Quaked with each Amen! Born of many
Sundays of prayer. I recall you patting
My head gently after the service intoning –
"Son, you too will become a man,"
My face beaming with pride.

(ii)

From the house where you lived
The twilight years of your life
We proceeded to the cemetery
By the old courthouse, your final

Resting place. You who nurtured us,
Made us see the wonders of sunsets
Siblings growing up tender years ago.

Your life large in magnanimity
Your soul sincere, you took branches
Of our clan under your wing. This,
You insisted, is how we ought to live -
Reaching out to others and being at
Peace with ourselves, even in the midst
Of life's upheavals, the grind of day by day.

Difficult as it may, this parting of mother
And son, I still find myself like the bookish
Five-year old, searching for your wisdom
As other people search for rare gems. Despite
The sadness of your passing, I am emboldened
By the maternal kindness and benevolence
That filled the home, a constant theme of your lifetime.

IV. Telling Tales

Chichiri 3pm
>   for Lloyd Muhara, Max Mbendera
>   and Dyborn Chibonga.

Walking home from Chichiri Secondary School
Our day having begun with Maths and Science,
And morning break watching dogs, first the sniffing.
Then hind leg raised, pissing at telephone poles
The dog piss seasoning the wood-

We bemoaned the June-July lunch time hours
Spent rehearsing Independence Day rallies.
Remember how they made us stand still
Straight, chin up, chest out, arms by the side,
On parade grounds, the Instructors barking orders
Synchronising drill steps to an accompaniment
Of a drum beat before the full brass band?

Stopping at Kamba market for boiled groundnuts,
Cassava and sugarcane, we moaned the rehearsals
Upsetting homework. Still, chewing the succulent cane
Sweetly, the juices streaming, tattooing our cheeks;
Thoughts of mock M.C.E exams; the same Maths
And Science loomed large in our heads.

Telling Tales

Legend has it that game hunters and wood collectors
Told tales of *Dziombam'nuzu* forest reserve enough to fill
One with greatest fright. They told and retold tales of
Woodland trees whistling ghostly tunes in the wilderness,
Of overripe pods spitting seeds loudly, self sowing. Men
Returning from the forest talked about man-eating beasts
On all fours roaming the plains; and how baboons smile
Before the kill. They recounted tales of spiders the size
Of crabs parachuting from treetops, and scorpions tails like
Exclamation marks, blood-red with venom, they said. Then
One mid-August day, gale-force winds ripped the forest
To its bark, sending tree mammals scuttling down for cover.
In the aftermath with no trees sighing, no birds calling, the loss
Of fauna and flora starkly apparent; the village rushed to see
Man-eating animals, giant spiders and scorpions. But found
Lifeless squirrels and mangled saplings littering the floor instead.
Today, men and women of the village disregard the hunter's
Tales and trust their eyes more.

The Granaries at Kanengo
    after severe drought, Malawi 2002

Even on this early December morning
The heat is on. And for many mornings
Before, the flaming sun baking the land
Bleaches acres of crops into lifeless yellow,
Scorching young maize to the roots.

Up and down the country, farmers soaking
The earth with sweat, toiling for their *nsima*,
Explain to TV cameras how, rainy seasons ago
Their fields teemed with cowpeas and beans.
How emerald green maize wearing pumpkin
Tendrils, elbowed for light towards harvest.

Elsewhere, town dwellers who saw a bumper year
In silver silos now talk of granaries standing
Hot and empty. Whispers doing the rounds
In barbershops and the rumour mill, hint
At petty bourgeois with an eye on commerce
And the business of business-as-usual, coming alive,
Auctioning National Grain to pay the National Debt?

The Mtondo Trees of Mangochi, 1981

Under the deep shade of outspread *Mtondo* trees
Tireless elders sat on ceremonial stools, in jury and
Judgment of village cases, surrounded by onlookers.
The onlookers silent as if studying the ceremony,
Their thoughts kept to themselves like a dirty secret
While the elder's core wisdom dispensed verdicts.

On other days, I witnessed medicine men squatting
On goat-skins, carefully arranging herbal cures
Like fragile furniture. Ailing men, women and
Children queuing, eyed hyena tails, castor-oil,
Sweet love potions and bitter root concoctions,

And waited patiently, hoping to hear
How, at the medicine-man's command
Might the hyena tails, herbs and oils
Arrest chronic fevers and pains running
Like malarial rivers in their veins; or how
The love potions might ignite their love life.

After dusk, the trees provided cover
For the placid nightlife of squirrels and
Gecko lizards dozing in moonless night.
That was then. Today I've come to see
The peninsula stripped of its evergreen
Trees; testament to the ways of man.

One season, in a wanton act, men clutching
Chainsaws hacked down colossal *Mtondo*
Trees to feed sawmills in the city, and
(Listening to leaf rumours), as choice wood
In timber yards and shops in far away lands
Beyond the oceans that bound this continent.

Today, with the trees cut and trucked away
The peninsula is cluttered by tree stumps
With roots dead in the soil. And I rest my
Troubled eyes on distant horizons where once
Mtondo trees stood tall, oxygenating the air.

The Cenotaph on Chipembere Highway

Two steps forward
Three steps back.
Bow-bent men
Weighed down by medals
And two World Wars
In their bones
Take a solemn bow
Before a slab
Of reinforced concrete
Built in the shape
Of a grinding stone.
And gathered here
In army khaki fatigues
Are those who survived to tell the tale
The men who fought two World Wars
In far outposts, made sacrifices oceans away
In Burma, India and Malaya; nouns
Compiled from places they went
The wars they fought
And fight they did, for King and Empire.
But after the dead empire
After several November parades
And time slowing their hands and legs
They must surely wonder if their valour -
The rapid fire that lit the trenches over *There*
Advanced their freedom over *Here*.

Those Makungwa Nights

Moonstruck, we went out excitedly
Into a moonlit vista, the moon luminous
The night flaunting her jewels, the stars.
One foot on the gas pedal, thick cloud of
Exhaust smoke trailing us we were off
To Makungwa bar, Kabula's hot spot.

Outside the bar, patrons sharing dry humour
Quenched voracious appetites with fried
Chicken wings, necks and thighs. The love
Of charcoal grilled chicken, jukebox music,
Beer and bar girls brought union of minds here.

Inside the bar, faces half-lit with stiff drinks
Rocked to the sound of vinyl; men and women
On the dance floor, coupling, in love with themselves,
In love with Rumba music. And the dancing -
A vertical expression of horizontal desire.

Visiting Maone
   for Nduna Mtalimanja

For me it all began here, my serious concentration
On the printed page, the power of the word. Living
In a nest of books, the retina expanding with every
Page of theorems, facts and figures; I was eager
To swallow all arts and sciences, propelled by
Expectations from parents, colleagues and village folk.

Leafing through books full of knowledge; the volume
Dial on the radio turned low, ear friendly music graced
The study room. On the radio DJ James Chimera announcing
Himself flooded the airwaves with local music: Robert Fumulani
And Mudi River Jazz Band, Nangalembe and The Kachamba
Brothers, punctuated by Mahotella Queens from *eGoli*.

The young today seem fearful for their future, less certain
Of the fruits of educating their precious brain. Less certain
Of their place in a world changing rapidly. Positive words
Lump in their throats. So, in the afterglow of several dawns
And half-truths, borrowed tongues and mannerisms; where
One is neither here nor there, shouldn't we open their eyes
To knowledge? Open their inquiring minds so that they
Walk not blind as moles? And shouldn't we show them
The riches of a future still lying ahead and not behind?

Not I

Weren't you born at noon
In the lunar year of the horse
A tiny body
Kicking and screaming
A vigorous statement
Of your arrival,
Wearing out
Your mother's patience
In the tropical heat
Of October sun?

Didn't you boast
About intercepting
A viper lunging
At an absent-minded
Rodent for its midday meal,
Fishing in rivers
Teeming with crocodiles
And beating a path through
Thorny acacia bushes?

Didn't you trek
Across mighty Zambezi
Thirsting for a better future,
Endure freezing winters overseas
For more letters after your name?

Could it be you now
Wearing worried looks
Staring at the world
With negative confidence
And in difficulty coordinating
Speech and thought?

Not I

The Flood, Mozambique; February 2000

Cumulus clouds above southern Africa
Explode into a downpour. Each
Raindrop spills the seeds of destruction
Across swathes of geography plagued by
First rains of the millennium.

Spattering rains and ocean winds gusting
Converge overland into cyclone *Eline*,
Flattening bamboo huts, uprooting
Sizzling pylons and telegraph poles,
Tossing livestock like toys in its wake.

Bridges sag under the burden. Umbrella
Canopied trees, in whose shade men
Sat carving traditional hoe handles
And sharing gourdfuls of millet beer, swirl.

For weeks, rain-filled days and nights
Turn greening fields into an inland sea.
Where cheerful communities once drowned
In the noise of life; now stillness
Blankets corpses pregnant with rainwater.

A helicopter, rustling its wings above mutinous
Limpopo and Zambezi in flood, veers close
To the nerve ends of wind-battered treetops
Like mechanical fruit harvester, plucks
Fatigued mother and her newborn
Away from the hell around them.

Touched with hope, a window of joy in Mozambique
Opens. But which village sage remembers mothers
Fathers, children, chickens, cats and dogs, wet
To the bone, huddled in eternal supplication?

Facing Zomba Plateau

Out of *Chingwe's* hole
Ancestral voices throng the veins
And lanes of Zomba plateau.
Generational voices of an earlier time;
Of lives broken and jettisoned
Taking their histories with them
Into *Chingwe's* hole, a cave of burials.
And now skeleton of words
Come echoing back from a rack of
Bones, long-laid, lodged like arrowheads
In confined deep clay, pouring forth their sad tale,
A harrowing reminder of modern day
Bosnia, Darfur and Rwanda. Lives
Disfigured by the horrors of undeclared wars.

Today, the funeral clouds
That shut all eyes to *Chingwe's* hole
Have cleared; and the monstrous dungeon
That crushed people's bones
Once, spilling their blood into rivers below
Is welcoming to visitors visiting a breath-taking
Plateau, genteel and hospitable, populated
By evergreen trees, the temples of chlorophyll.

Notes and Glossary

Alpeteshie	A strong traditional gin from Ghana
Beni	A military-style traditional dance of Yao men and women.
Bonongwe	*Amaranthus spp*, a tasty vegetable grown for its leaves.
Chambo	A delicious and popular fish found in lake Malawi.
Chewa	One of the main Bantu groups of Malawi concentrated in the country's central region. And according historical records, they form part of the Luba-Lunda Migration from what is Now the Democratic Republic of Congo. The language Spoken by the group is called Chichewa.
Chibuku	Commercial beer brewed in Southern Africa.
Chigawe	Old name for Mangochi District site, Malawi.
Chingwe's Hole	A hole on Zomba plateau into which, according to legend, Wrong-doers were thrown. Zomba Town, once the capital of Malawi is situated at the foot of the plateau as well as Chancellor College, the main university campus.
Chiperoni	A cold, south-easterly wind that brings rain to parts of Southern Malawi, during the months of June and July.
Chitenje	Printed fabric
Dambwe	Area in the forest where members of Gule Wamkulu (Big Dance) gather before and after the dance.
Dimba	Gardens that utilise residual moisture after rain season, also Refers to off-season gardening along watercourses like rivers And streams.
Dziombam'nuzu	Literally means 'whistling or singing forest'. A Dense Woodland found in the lakeshore area of Nankumba Peninsula, Mangochi, part of Lake Malawi National Park. A World Heritage Site.
eGoli.	Zulu word for 'City of Gold,' now Johannesburg.
Fufu	Ghanaian word for hard porridge made from cassava.
Funwe	A mountain in Mangochi, dominates Nankumba Peninsula.
Kafula	Original inhabitants of Malawi also known as Abatwa.
Kabula	The old name for the present day commercial city of Blantyre, Malawi. Versions of the origin of the name exist: One version refers to a Yao Chief by the same name, who Successfully defended his fiefdom against outside invaders. A Different version cites Kabula Hill in Blantyre as the origin.
Kwela	Literally means 'to climb' or 'to go up' in Zulu. Since the

	Fifties and sixties the word has been associated with popular urban music style of Southern Africa.
Masuku	*Uapaca kirkiana* (African Loquat), fruits are borne in Clusters and when fully ripe, they are brown, fleshy and juicy. The tree fruits extremely heavily and is a symbol of fertility for The Bemba people of Zambia.
m'Bida	Delicious leaf vegetable also known as 'Choumollier' in Zimbabwe.
Mfutso	Vegetables, often half-cooked, sun dried and stored for consumption during out of season months.
Mtondo	Tall, shady tree (*Afzelia quanzensis*) found in low lying areas of Malawi.
Ngoni	Descendants of Zulu people of South Africa, found in parts of Malawi, Zambia, Zimbabwe and Mozambique.
Nsima	Hard porridge prepared from maize and millet flour.
Ingoma	A warrior dance of Ngoni people of Malawi.
Phirilongwe	A range of hills in Mvumba Village, Mangochi.
Sadza	cf. Nsima.
Thobwa	Nutritious drink made from millet and maize.

The poem 'Another Winter,' appears in its draft form in *Operations and Tears, New Malawi Anthology* under the title 'Letter from Abroad.' The version in this collection is final and definitive.

www.ingramcontent.com/pod-product-compliance
Lightning Source LLC
Chambersburg PA
CBHW021848220426
43663CB00005B/451